ON THE FARM

Susie Behar

Illustrated by Essi Kimpimäki

Kane Miller
A DIVISION OF EDC PUBLISHING

Our farmer is busy all year round.

She has lots of plants and animals to care for,
from apple trees to cows and chickens.
Other nearby farmers grow crops
such as flowers, pumpkins and corn.

Shine a flashlight behind the page, or hold
it up to the light to reveal what is hidden
in and around all these farms.
Discover a world of great surprises.

It's winter on our farm and our farmer has put hay into a feeder for her animals to eat.

Can you see which animals are eating the hay?

Munch!
Munch!

Cows are eating the hay.

They need the extra food when
the grass is covered by snow.

Brrr! It's cold today. Many of the animals on our farm are staying inside to keep warm.

Who lives in this shelter?

A female pig, called
a sow, lives in this pigsty.
She has a litter of eight
piglets to look after.

The piglets are huddled
together in the straw
next to their mother.

Snuffle!
Oink!

Close to our farm, there is a larger farm
that has lots of big buildings, including
a farmhouse and barns and stables
for the animals.

There is also a tall tower
called a silo.

Shall we take a peek inside?

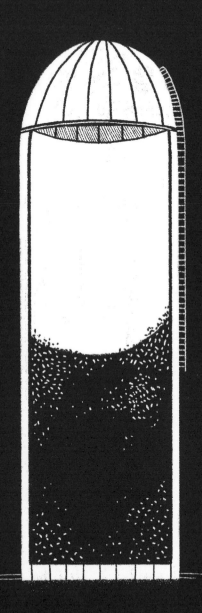

The silo is full of grain
that the farmer
harvested in the fall.

The farmer stores
it in the silo so that
it stays fresh and dry.
The grain is used to feed
the animals in winter.

It's spring and lots of baby animals are being born on our farm. The vet has come to check on a new arrival.

What do you think the vet is doing?

The vet is listening to the foal's heartbeat to make sure she is healthy. He will also check that the mother is well.

Ba-boom!

Ba-boom!

A ewe gave birth to three lambs in the night. One is snuggling up to her mother to drink milk and one is sleeping.

Where is the third lamb?

Here he is!

Our farmer is feeding him
milk from a bottle. Sometimes,
the ewe is unable to feed
all her lambs herself.

Glug!
Glug!

A coop is a small building where chickens are kept.

This hen is settling down for the night in her coop. Is she alone?

No. Her chicks are nestled under her wings.
This keeps them safe and warm.

Cheep!

Cheep!

This farmer is busy growing
flowers to sell.

Shall we see where
they are growing?

The flowers are
growing inside
a hoop house,
a tunnel made
from plastic.

The hoop house lets in
sunlight, but keeps
the flowers safe
from wind, which
could bend or break
their stems.

It's summer, and our farmer is growing vegetables. There is a big vegetable garden on our farm.

Can you see which vegetables are growing in the soil?

There are carrots,
onions and potatoes.

These are root vegetables
that grow beneath
the ground.

A group of schoolchildren are visiting our farm to learn about the animals and plants.

What are they learning about now?

They are watching our farmer milk a cow.

The milk is gently squeezed out of the cow's udder and is collected in a bucket.

Splish!
Splash!

On another nearby farm, a farmer is harvesting his hay. A machine called a hay baler turns the cut hay into round bales.

How does it do this?

The hay baler has lots of rollers
that collect and shape the hay.

Hay bales keep
the hay fresh
and are easy
to store.

whirr!
whirr!

Summer is turning into fall.
In the orchard on our farm, the apple
trees are laden with delicious fruit.
It's time to fill boxes with ripe apples.

Who is picking
the apples?

There are lots of people picking the apples. Some have come to work on our farm for the apple harvest. They will leave once the apples have all been picked.

Our farmer and her family help with the apple harvest too.

This local farm grows different types of crops. Corn is planted in the Spring, grows tall in the Summer and is harvested in the fall.

Where is the part of the corn that we eat?

Here it is!

It grows inside
the leafy
husks.

Rustle!
Rustle!

High above
the corn field,
a farmer has
placed a nest
box in a tree.

Can you
see who's
inside?

It's a barn owl!

The farmer has given the owl a home on the farm. The owl hunts the mice that eat the farmer's crops. The owl is nocturnal and hunts at night.

Shhh! Shhh!

Late in fall, the fields
of this pumpkin farm
are looking empty.

Where are all
the pumpkins?

The pumpkins are in the trailer.

They have been harvested
and are ready to be taken
to the stores and markets,
where they will be sold.

The harvest is over and our farmer is at the farmers' market. She is selling onion chutney and applesauce.

What else do you think she has for sale at the market today?

She is selling things from her neighbors' farms, too. There are potatoes, eggs, corn, carrots, pumpkins, flowers and apples.

Farmers work hard to make sure everything goes well on their farms.

Every day is a busy day on a farm.

There's more...

Take a closer look around the farm.

Dairy farming Farmers keep dairy cows for their milk. The cows are milked several times a day. The milk can be drunk or used to make butter, cheese and yogurt.

Tractors Tractors are vehicles that can pull heavy loads. They have powerful engines, but this power is used to pull tools or machines, rather than for speed. On a farm, tractors are used to pull hay balers, plows and trailers.

Scarecrows Scarecrows are used to scare birds away from fields where crops are growing so that the crops do not get eaten by the birds. It is thought that the first people to use scarecrows were the Ancient Egyptians (more than 3,000 years ago). They placed them on the banks of the River Nile to protect their wheat crops.

Barns Farmers store hay and farm machinery in barns. Animals, such as cows, pigs, chickens, horses, sheep, goats and donkeys, are also kept in barns. If it is cold or raining, barns are a safe place for animals to shelter or sleep.

Farm vets Farm vets work with animals such as horses, sheep, pigs and cows. They can help farmers when animals are giving birth, tend to sick animals and vaccinate animals against diseases.

Hay Hay is grass that has been cut and dried. Farmers use it as an animal feed for grazing animals such as cows, horses, goats and sheep. Straw is different from hay—it's made from the leftover stalks of crops and is usually used as animal bedding.

Produce Lots of our foodstuffs, such as cereals, bread and vegetables, come from crops grown on farms. Farmers sell their produce to supermarkets and stores, as well as at local farmers' markets.

First American Edition 2018
Kane Miller, A Division of EDC Publishing

Copyright © 2018 Quarto Publishing plc

Published by arrangement with Ivy Kids, an imprint of The Quarto Group.

For information contact:
Kane Miller, A Division of EDC Publishing
PO Box 470663
Tulsa, OK 74147-0663
www.kanemiller.com
www.edcpub.com
www.usbornebooksandmore.com

Library of Congress Control Number: 2017942238
Printed in China

ISBN: 978-1-61067-665-6